Original title:
The Dreamy Doodle Pad

Copyright © 2024 Creative Arts Management OÜ
All rights reserved.

Author: Olivia Sterling
ISBN HARDBACK: 978-9916-90-494-7
ISBN PAPERBACK: 978-9916-90-495-4

Charcoal Clouds

Darkness drapes the evening sky,
The charcoal clouds begin to sigh.
Whispers travel through the air,
Like secrets tangled in despair.

Thunder rumbles, fierce and deep,
Awakening the night from sleep.
Lightening flickers, sharp and bright,
Illuminating the restless night.

Raindrops dance on trembling leaves,
Nature sings, the heart believes.
Each drop a story, wild and free,
As storms labor to set things free.

Illusions and Ink

In the margins of the page,
Words collide as thoughts engage.
Lines entwined with dreams and fears,
Bottled ink flows through the years.

Illustrations of a thousand sights,
Painted echoes, silent flights.
Illusions whisper in the void,
Where hopes and doubts are oft deployed.

Textures blend, the feel of time,
In ink we weave our quiet rhyme.
Captured moments, fleeting, grand,
Life's verses written in the sand.

Harmony in Hues

Colors swirl in gentle dance,
Each stroke a fleeting, vivid chance.
Palette rich with dreams untold,
Whispers of the heart unfold.

Beneath the sun's warm golden glow,
Rivers of emotion flow.
Shades of blue, a calming breath,
In every hue, we find the depth.

Painting worlds with brush and soul,
Together they make a vibrant whole.
Harmony sings in every tone,
In this canvas, we're never alone.

Reverberations of Reverie

Silent echoes dance and sway,
In reverie, we drift away.
Thoughts like shadows, soft and light,
Bathe our souls in dream's delight.

As starlit whispers weave the night,
Imagination takes to flight.
Waves of memory crash and swell,
Each moment a story to tell.

Time bends gently in this space,
Held in dreams, we find our grace.
Reverberations of what could be,
In this realm, we're wild and free.

Vivid Visions

In bursts of color, dreams unfold,
With whispers bright, the tales retold.
A world alive with radiant light,
Each stroke of brush ignites the night.

The canvas breathes, each hue a sigh,
Explorations soar, our spirits fly.
In twilight's grip, we lose our way,
Yet find a joy that holds its sway.

Minds unbound by limits thin,
We dance the line of where we've been.
With every glance, new stories bloom,
In vivid realms, we carve the gloom.

Depths of thought, forgotten lore,
In vibrant flashes, we explore.
Awakening within a dream,
Where visions pulse and colors gleam.

Echoes of Imagination

Whispers linger in the air,
Moments captured, laid so bare.
A thought, a spark, a journey starts,
In wondrous realms, we play our parts.

Time transcends with every blend,
Waves of sound that twist and bend.
In echoes rich, our voices call,
An endless dance where shadows fall.

From distant shores, the stories flow,
Through winding paths, where dreams do grow.
Imagination's flares ignite,
Revealing secrets wrapped in night.

A symphony of hopes and fears,
In every note, the heart's own tears.
With open minds, we seek to find,
The magic held within the mind.

Palette of Fantasies

A canvas large, a dreamer's space,
With shades and tints, we dare to trace.
From softest blues to fiery red,
Each stroke of thought, a path we tread.

In fantasy, the heart takes flight,
In realms unseen, they bask in light.
From tangled woods, to skies of gold,
The stories of the brave unfold.

With painter's hands, we craft the scene,
Each vibrant hue a whispered dream.
Together woven, threads of fate,
In the palette, we create.

A world where wishes freely roam,
In crafted tales, we find our home.
Colors dance in joyous glee,
A testament to what can be.

Dreamscapes in Graphite

In shades of gray, the visions unfold,
With pencil strokes, the dreams retold.
A world constructed, line by line,
Within the shadows, magic twines.

From fleeting thoughts, to places wide,
Each whisper of graphite, a tide.
In stillness found within the art,
We capture glimpses of the heart.

With sharpened tips, the stories weave,
A tapestry of what we believe.
In every shadow, light will peek,
Exploring depths, we dare to seek.

In quiet realms of charcoal dreams,
Life stirs with hushed and tender themes.
Through pencil's dance, we see the night,
Where each creation finds its flight.

Tales Told in Lines

In whispered words, stories arise,
From ink and paper, no disguise.
Each stroke a journey, lost and found,
In every line, where dreams abound.

Through winding paths, we take our flight,
In daylight's gleam and the moon's light.
Ancient legends, softly spun,
Play out their tales, one by one.

From forest deep to mountain high,
Each page a spark, a reason why.
Within these lines, our voices blend,
A tapestry that will not end.

In echoes sweet, the past will call,
As shadows dance upon the wall.
These tales we tell, a treasure chest,
In every line, our hearts at rest.

Dreamlike Depths

In twilight's haze, the visions bloom,
Soft shadows weave, dispelling gloom.
A gentle sigh, the world asleep,
In silent depths, our dreams we keep.

Like rivers flowing, thoughts take flight,
Across the canvas of the night.
Whispers mirror what we hold dear,
In dreamlike realms, we shed each fear.

Stars become the paint we wield,
In cosmic fields, our hearts revealed.
We dance on clouds, in colors bright,
Embracing all, the dark and light.

Through shifting mists, we find our way,
In dreamlike depths, forever sway.
Reality fades like morning dew,
As visions lead, we start anew.

Scribbles of Solitude

In solitude's grasp, my pen does roam,
Across the page, I find my home.
Each scribbled thought, a fleeting friend,
In quiet corners, my heart will mend.

Frayed edges whisper, secrets bare,
Untold stories woven with care.
A canvas filled with hues of gray,
In solitude's veil, I drift away.

Thoughts collide like a winter's freeze,
In gentle strokes, I feel at ease.
Every shadow holds a light,
In scribbles of solitude, I ignite.

The echoes linger, softly sound,
In every mark, a world profound.
Alone yet whole, I pen my creed,
In sacred silence, the soul is freed.

Thoughts in Technicolor

In vivid hues, thoughts come alive,
Each color bursts, where dreams arrive.
A palette rich with hopes and fears,
In technicolor, we shift the gears.

From golden rays to azure skies,
In every shade, a truth that lies.
Brush strokes dance upon the page,
In technicolor, we disengage.

Moments captured, bright and bold,
In stories told, our hearts unfold.
Each vibrant thought a puzzle piece,
In technicolor, we find our peace.

Through swirling shades, we find our voice,
In every hue, we make our choice.
Expressing life in every tone,
Thoughts in technicolor, never alone.

Paintbrush Poetics

In hues of dreams, the colors play,
Each stroke a thought, in light of day.
Whispers of art in every line,
A canvas world, where spirits shine.

Palette spills where shadows blend,
Creating worlds that never end.
With every touch, emotions flow,
A painted heart, a vibrant glow.

Shapes emerge from silence deep,
Where visions dance and memories keep.
Textures weave in bold embrace,
Crafting stories time can't erase.

In every shade, a tale unfolds,
Of whispered dreams and secrets told.
Life's canvas breathes, alive and bright,
An artful journey, pure delight.

Wistful Whispers

In twilight's hush, the shadows sigh,
Fleeting moments drift and fly.
Echoes of laughter, soft and clear,
In sacred spaces, we hold dear.

Memories linger, sweet yet faint,
Like gentle brushstrokes, they'll not taint.
A whisper's warmth, a tender glance,
In quiet corners, hearts still dance.

Through veils of time, we surely weave,
Tales of love that we believe.
Wistful dreams in starlit nights,
Guide our souls to golden heights.

In the silence, voices meld,
Stories of hope and joy upheld.
With every sigh, a wish takes flight,
Wistful whispers fade to light.

Vibrant Vignettes

In bustling streets, life's colors blend,
Each moment captured, a story penned.
Fleeting smiles, like rays of sun,
Vibrant vignettes, each one a run.

Dancing leaves in autumn's breath,
Whispers of life, even in death.
A child's laughter fills the air,
Moments of joy that we can share.

Through framed reflections, we explore,
The beauty found in what's in store.
Each snapshot holds a tale untold,
In vibrant hues, our lives unfold.

Time slips by, like grains of sand,
Yet in these vignettes, we will stand.
Memories linger, bright and true,
Vibrant glimpses, forever new.

The Language of Lines

In every curve, stories reside,
A dance of ink, a faithful guide.
Lines that twist, and some that flow,
The language of lines, a world to show.

Each stroke whispers secrets untold,
Of battles fought and dreams bold.
Flowing freely, they intertwine,
Creating paths in the grand design.

In black and white, or colors bright,
The language transcends, ignites the night.
Through tangled webs, or straight and true,
Lines lead us onward, me and you.

So let us pen our tales in ink,
With every line, a chance to think.
In the language of lines, we'll align,
Crafting our stories, your heart with mine.

Celestial Scribbles

In the sky, stars gently twinkle,
Drawing dreams with silver ink.
Clouds drift softly through the night,
Creating shapes that make us think.

Whispers of the moonlight glow,
Painting shadows on the ground.
Each constellation tells a tale,
In the stillness, magic found.

Across the vast and endless space,
Galaxies spin in a dance of light.
Invisible threads connect us all,
In this cosmic tapestry so bright.

With every heartbeat, we explore,
The mysteries above our heads.
Celestial scribbles guide our souls,
In their light, our hope embeds.

The Realm of Swirls

In the realm where colors blend,
Swirls of wonder paint the air.
Thoughts like rivers flow and bend,
Carrying dreams beyond compare.

Every curve has a story told,
Whirling shadows, bright and bold.
In this dance, our spirits meet,
Embracing chaos, bittersweet.

Patterns form and lose their way,
A tapestry of fleeting grace.
Lost in spirals, we find the play,
In every turn, a soft embrace.

In the heart of swirling skies,
We discover what it means to feel.
In this realm where freedom lies,
Our minds awaken, and we heal.

Tangles of Thought

In the labyrinth of the mind,
Threads of reason intertwine.
Tangles of thought, so hard to find,
Seeking clarity, a silver line.

Worries spin in tangled knots,
Joy and sorrow, mixed and curled.
In this chaos, we connect the dots,
As we navigate our winding world.

Each idea, a ribbon bright,
Twisting in the gentle breeze.
Unraveling secrets in the night,
Finding solace in the tease.

Through the maze, we learn to cope,
Understanding bends and weaves.
In these tangles, we find hope,
A tapestry of hearts that believes.

Ethereal Sketches

With a gentle touch of grace,
Ethereal sketches fill the air.
Lines and strokes that softly trace,
Moments caught, forever rare.

Whispers of the fading light,
Brushstrokes echo on the ground.
In the stillness of the night,
Artistry in dreams profound.

Each sketch a glimpse of what could be,
Infinite stories left to tell.
In every shadow, we can see,
Magic hidden, casting spells.

Through the realm of fleeting sights,
We capture beauty, pure and bright.
Ethereal sketches, a dance divine,
In our hearts, their warmth will shine.

Kaleidoscope of Dreams

Colors swirl and dance so bright,
Whispers of the stars at night.
Each turn reveals a brand new scene,
Shifting shapes in worlds unseen.

Waves of hope crash on the shores,
Endless paths with open doors.
Every shadow tells a tale,
In this realm, we shall not fail.

Visions blend like paints on glass,
Moments fleeting, yet they last.
Hearts aligned with beating drums,
In this place, eternity comes.

Dreamers wander, hand in hand,
In a world of soft, grainy sand.
Weave our stories, bright and bold,
In the dreams that we behold.

Penumbra of Possibilities

In the twilight where shadows play,
Choices linger, lost in sway.
Whispers of what might unfold,
In the shadows, secrets told.

Fleeting moments dance and tease,
Life's a puzzle, pieces breeze.
Every step a choice to make,
In the dusk, our paths awake.

Misty views and shadows blend,
Paths unknown around the bend.
Hope ignites like stars in dark,
In this realm, we leave a mark.

Dare to dream, and dare to seek,
In the silence, hear the peak.
Endless journeys, wide and free,
In the penumbra, we shall be.

Doodles of Dusk

Sketches linger on the page,
As the sun begins to age.
Pencil strokes of fleeting time,
Ink that flows in rhythm and rhyme.

Colors fade into the night,
Whispers of the day take flight.
Nights adorned with starry specks,
Every doodle, dear effects.

Imagination starts to thrive,
In the twilight, thoughts alive.
Lines intertwine in gentle curves,
In these dreams, the heart observes.

Every doodle tells a tale,
Bringing joy when shadows pale.
In this art, we laugh and play,
Creating worlds in a soft gray.

Flights of Fancy

In a feathered, soft embrace,
We ascend through dream's vast space.
Wings of hope that lift so high,
Chasing clouds that drift and sigh.

Whispers swirl on breezy streams,
Carrying our wildest dreams.
Every flutter, every spin,
In the heart, the journey begins.

From the ground, we rise and twirl,
In the sky, our thoughts unfurl.
Boundless skies, horizons wide,
In this journey, we confide.

Flights that take us far away,
In the twilight's golden ray.
Chase the stars, embrace the night,
In our fancies, we find light.

Misty Reveries

In the haze of morning light,
Whispers dance on dew-kissed grass.
Dreams unfurl in gentle flight,
As time within the mist does pass.

Veils of fog like secrets loom,
Nature's breath, a soft embrace.
Echoes linger, shadows bloom,
Lost in this enchanted space.

Thoughts drift like the silent tide,
Merging with the quiet night.
In stillness, souls will abide,
Finding peace where dreams take flight.

Inked Adventures

With pen in hand, worlds collide,
Imagination knows no bounds.
Each stroke a journey to decide,
As ink spills forth on paper grounds.

Characters leap, alive and bold,
Their tales woven with depth and care.
In every line, a story told,
Daring readers to venture there.

Maps of dreams across the page,
Wonders waiting to be found.
In whispered words, we engage,
Crafting visions that astound.

Whimsy on Paper

A sprinkle of joy on every line,
Colors burst like laughter's song.
In doodles and sketches, I find,
A world where we all belong.

Playful thoughts like children run,
Chasing shadows, dancing free.
In this realm, we share the fun,
Creating what is yet to be.

With whimsy wrapped in each design,
Imagination finds its way.
In paper dreams, our hearts entwine,
As we craft our perfect day.

Fragments of Flight

A feather's fall, a breeze that sighs,
Moments captured in a glance.
With every heartbeat, hope still flies,
Inviting us to take a chance.

Clouds drift softly, thoughts arise,
Sketching stories in the sky.
The horizon calls, a sweet surprise,
Through open wings, we learn to fly.

In fragments of a daydream's height,
We weave our wishes on the loom.
With courage drawn from starlit night,
We soar above, dispelling gloom.

Fantastical Fractals

Shapes unfold in wild design,
Patterns dance, a grand divine.
Each twist a secret to behold,
A universe in form untold.

Colors blend, a vibrant song,
In these forms, we all belong.
Infinity in a single glance,
Geometry's enchanting dance.

Growing ever, ever more,
Patterns rich, we can explore.
In the chaos, find the grace,
Fractals weave in time and space.

From tiny seeds, worlds emerge,
In nature's beauty, we converge.
Mirrored wonders, sights enthrall,
In fractals' charm, we find our call.

Shadows and Strokes

In twilight's hush, shadows creep,
Brushstrokes whisper, secrets keep.
Canvas blank, a world awaits,
With every stroke, life conversates.

Colors blend, dusk's embrace,
Artistry in shadows' grace.
Whispers of the night unfold,
Stories painted, bold and gold.

Each shadow tells a tale of old,
Through every hue, dreams are sold.
In quiet nooks where echoes play,
Life's canvas paints night and day.

With every stroke, a heart beats clear,
Art reveals what eyes can't hear.
In shadows deep, the truth awakes,
The magic lies in all it makes.

Embers of Enchantment

In the hearth of flick'ring light,
Embers dance, a warming sight.
Stories whisper from the flame,
Magic lives in the untamed.

Glowing coals, a gentle glow,
Flickering dreams in night's flow.
Each spark a wish, a hope, a prayer,
In smoky wisps, we wander where.

The night's embrace, a cloak of stars,
Sharing tales of near and far.
Amidst the crackle, life ignites,
In every ember, pure delight.

So gather close, let warmth unite,
Through shadows deep, our hearts take flight.
For in this glow, enchantment lies,
In every spark, our spirits rise.

Echoes of the Unseen

Whispers linger in the air,
Echoes of the dreams we bear.
Silent songs of days gone past,
In fleeting shadows, hearts hold fast.

Waves of time, an unseen thread,
Where fears and hopes are gently fed.
Every sigh, a soft refrain,
Carried forth like gentle rain.

Through the mist of memories lost,
Life's sweet echoes, never tossed.
In the silence, truths abide,
In every wave, we find our guide.

So listen close, for you may find,
The echoes of the heart and mind.
In the stillness, beauty reigns,
In whispers soft, love remains.

Imaginative Echoes in Hue

In a world where colors blend,
Dreams unfurl, and visions bend.
Brushstrokes dance, wild and free,
A canvas painted, just to be.

Whispers soft in every shade,
Voices linger, memories made.
Every hue a tale to tell,
In the silence, echoes dwell.

In violet skies and golden seas,
The heart finds peace, the spirit flees.
Imagination leaps and soars,
Unlocking dreams behind closed doors.

A tapestry of light and sound,
In this wonder, we are bound.
Each echo breathing life anew,
In the symphony of every hue.

Uncharted Territory of Dreams

Wandering through the night's embrace,
In dreams we find a secret place.
Where shadows play and laughter twirls,
A realm of magic, dreams unfurl.

The stars compose a quiet tune,
Beneath the glow of a silver moon.
Each step we take, we come alive,
In uncharted lands, we thrive.

With hearts unbound, we chase the light,
Into the depths of the endless night.
Awake, we breathe, in this vast sea,
Exploring what it means to be free.

The journey calls, with open arms,
A treasure trove of hidden charms.
In dreams we sail, in dreams we roam,
Finding within, a place called home.

Whispers of Stardust

In the quiet of the evening glow,
A gentle breeze begins to flow.
Stars above, like diamonds bright,
Whisper secrets of the night.

Galaxies swirl in cosmic flight,
Echoing tales in the depth of night.
Every twinkle holds a sigh,
A longing heart, a wish to fly.

Softly falls the velvet sky,
Where dreams awaken, spirits fly.
In stardust trails, we find our place,
Infinite love in the vast embrace.

With every breath, the universe hums,
In the silence, magic comes.
Together, we'll chase the dawn,
Where stardust dreams are never gone.

Canvas of Clouds

A palette painted, soft and wide,
Clouds like whispers, dreams abide.
Shapes and shadows drift and blend,
Nature's art, where time transcends.

Above the world, the skies unfold,
Stories waiting to be told.
Each fiber floats, a fleeting glance,
In the dance of clouds, we take a chance.

From silver linings to hues of gray,
Feel the magic, come what may.
Every gust, a gentle sigh,
A canvas stretching, far and high.

In twilight's caress, the colors sway,
A breath of wonder at the close of day.
The sky's embrace, a calming shroud,
Life's reflections on a canvas of clouds.

Mystical Marks

In the night, secrets weave,
A tapestry that souls believe.
Whispers pulse in cosmic light,
Carving paths through silent night.

Branches stretch, the echoes call,
As the universe weaves its shawl.
Each mark a story, wide and deep,
In the silence, dreams we keep.

Dancing stars, twinkling bright,
Reveal truths nestled in the night.
Hands trace lines upon the sky,
Binding hearts as time drifts by.

Mystic symbols softly glow,
Guiding us where spirits flow.
In the realm where shadows play,
Marks of wonder light our way.

Brushstrokes of Bliss

With gentle hues, the canvas sings,
A splash of joy, the heart takes wings.
Colors blend in soft embrace,
Creating kindness in their grace.

Each brushstroke tells a vibrant tale,
Of laughter shared, of dreams set sail.
In the palette, life's sweet dance,
Invites all souls to take a chance.

From dusk till dawn, the visions flow,
Bright reminders of love's warm glow.
Together we create the art,
A masterpiece from every heart.

In every corner, beauty waits,
To paint the world with open gates.
With every stroke, we find our way,
Through brushstrokes of bliss, we'll sway.

The Dance of Doodles

Softly curling, lines entwine,
Creating worlds where dreams align.
With each doodle, thoughts run free,
Whispers of what we long to see.

Spirals twist, and figures leap,
Ink and paper secrets keep.
In the margins, magic sways,
Guiding hearts through quiet days.

Fleeting thoughts on paper cast,
In this dance, we're free at last.
With scribbled joy, we find our way,
In doodles bright, we long to stay.

Each sketch alive, a story told,
In doodles warm against the cold.
In this rhythm, pure and light,
We draw our dreams, we lose the night.

Shadows of the Mind

Whispers haunting, shadows play,
Traces linger where thoughts stray.
In the corners of our souls,
Echoes dance, the silence polls.

Veiled emotions, dark and bright,
Illuminate the endless night.
Secrets tucked in heartbeats' flow,
In the quiet, truths will grow.

Through the tempest, stillness calls,
In the shadows, wisdom sprawls.
Finding light in darkest space,
Shadows shift, transforming grace.

In the labyrinth where we roam,
Every shadow finds its home.
Through the mind's uncharted sea,
Shadows of truth will set us free.

Patterns of Passion

In shadows dance, two hearts entwined,
Whispers weave through twilight's sighs.
A tapestry of love designed,
Beneath the stars, where magic lies.

Fingers trace a fleeting dream,
Boldly wrapped in warmth's embrace.
Each moment glows, a vibrant beam,
In secret corners, time finds grace.

Lost within the gaze of night,
Echoing the silence sweet.
Every heartbeat, pure delight,
As passions rise and shadows meet.

With every glance, new worlds appear,
A symphony of souls in bloom.
In patterns rich, they draw us near,
Love's canvas woven, heart's own room.

The Heart's Sketchbook

Pages turn with gentle care,
Inked with dreams both bright and bold.
Each sketch a touch, a whispered prayer,
A story waiting to be told.

Lines that curve like lovers' sighs,
Hearts that leap and softly land.
With every stroke, the canvas cries,
A yearning touch of tender hand.

In colors bright, emotions flow,
Dancing across the paper's face.
A heart's desire, deeply we sow,
Capturing time, a fleeting grace.

When shadows fall, the light reveals,
The sketches drawn in dusk's embrace.
In this book, our soul conceals,
Every heartbeat, every trace.

Silken Strokes

With every brush upon the skin,
A whisper kindles, soft and light.
Strokes of silk where souls begin,
Awakening the endless night.

Fingers dance with gentle grace,
Tracing paths on silken dreams.
In this art, we find our place,
Where passion flows like silver streams.

Each touch ignites a flame unknown,
A spark that fuels, a sweet embrace.
In silken strokes, our love is shown,
Entwined in moments, time we chase.

Canvas bare, yet hearts are full,
In every line, a story blooms.
Silken threads that pull and pull,
Binding life in fragrant rooms.

Lightness of Being

In morning's glow, we breathe in deep,
The world awakes, a gentle sigh.
A dance of joy, a leap, a leap,
In lightness, spirits soar and fly.

The breeze whispers through every tree,
Nature's laughter fills the air.
We chase the sun, wild and free,
In simple moments, love we share.

With open hearts, we tread the skies,
Each step a song, a radiant call.
The lightness found in sweet goodbyes,
In fleeting shadows, we stand tall.

So let us glide on dreams of white,
Embracing joy, unbound, serene.
In every heartbeat, pure delight,
The lightness of our souls, unseen.

Surreal Shades

In twilight's grasp where shadows play,
Colors blend in odd array.
A whisper wrapped in mystic hues,
Dreams unfurl in vibrant views.

Beneath the moon, illusions sway,
Reality begins to fray.
Figures dance in muted light,
Chasing echoes through the night.

A landscape drawn in fractured lines,
Where thought and image intertwines.
The air is thick with painted sighs,
Beneath an ever-shifting sky.

Within this realm, where senses blend,
One finds a path that twists and bends.
Surreal shades that we embrace,
In the heart of time and space.

Dreamweaver's Canvas

Upon the loom of quiet sleep,
Threads of silver softly creep.
Patterns spun in soft embrace,
Crafting worlds where shadows trace.

Each dream a stroke, a vivid hue,
Shaping all that might come true.
In the folds of night's retreat,
The canvas blooms, both bright and sweet.

Wanderers lost in visions vast,
Chasing moments from the past.
Through colors rich and journeys wide,
The dreamweaver guides with gentle pride.

As dawn approaches, dreams take flight,
Fading softly into light.
Yet in the heart, the dreams remain,
Whispers of the night's sweet gain.

Tapestry of Tranquility

In silent woods where whispers rest,
A tapestry of peace is blessed.
Gentle streams and rustling leaves,
Weaving calm as nature breathes.

Each thread of sound, a soft decree,
Grants the soul its history.
A quiet song in nature's choir,
Lifts the spirit, sparks desire.

Beneath the sky's embracing dome,
Hearts unite, finding home.
With every breeze that stirs the air,
Joy and solace linger there.

In this sanctuary of light,
Every moment feels just right.
A tapestry of dreams unfurled,
Cradles softly our shared world.

Fluid Fantasies

In rivers deep where visions flow,
Fluid fantasies start to grow.
Ideas drift on currents wide,
Emotions swell like the turning tide.

A dance of light across the waves,
Each ripple whispers, gently saves.
In shifting forms, the stories wake,
An art of dreams the heart can make.

Stars above like scattered seeds,
Planting hope in liquid needs.
In every drop, a tale anew,
Fluid fantasies to guide us through.

As the night swallows the sun,
Each fantasy, a race now run.
Yet still they shimmer, bright and clear,
Fluid treasures we hold dear.

Echoes of a Dreamer's Sketch

In twilight's soft embrace they dance,
Sketching worlds in a fleeting glance.
Whispers of hopes in colors bright,
Awakening stars in the quiet night.

Floating on clouds of pastel schemes,
Carving out paths from fragile dreams.
Each stroke a wish on a shadowed page,
In the heart of silence, they gently wage.

Beneath the moon's soft, silver glow,
Visions bloom where wild thoughts flow.
A tapestry woven in starlit seams,
Echoes linger from the dreamer's themes.

Fractured thoughts in a gentle breeze,
Fleeting moments that aim to please.
In every dreamer's sketch, we find,
A piece of the soul, intertwined.

Scribbled Reveries

Amid the chaos of a restless mind,
Subtle stories in margins skinned.
With pen in hand, I chase the day,
Through scribbled lines where shadows play.

In the corners of a tattered page,
Whispers dance like a fleeting sage.
Each word a flicker, each dot a spark,
Lighting the canvas from dark to dark.

Reveries tumble like leaves in fall,
Captured thoughts that rise and stall.
A world unfolds with each inked trace,
Creating wonder in an empty space.

Scribbles turn to vivid tales,
Navigating life like paper sails.
In these margins, my heart takes flight,
Guided by dreams in the soft twilight.

Inked Visions from Sleep

From the depths where silence breathes,
Inked visions rise like autumn leaves.
Unfolding stories in shadows cast,
Through the night, their echoes last.

Softly painted with midnight hues,
Whispers float on the morning dews.
Each stroke a tale, each line a sigh,
A bridge to worlds where wishes lie.

In slumber's grasp, the thoughts collide,
Secrets weave like a gentle tide.
From dreams awakened, colors burst,
In inked visions, we quench our thirst.

With every dawn, they fade away,
Yet linger on like the light of day.
In quiet moments, we hold them dear,
Inked visions dance, forever near.

The Canvas of Wandering Dreams

In twilight's glow, a canvas sprawls,
Where wandering dreams flutter and call.
Each brushstroke whispers of tales untold,
A tapestry woven with threads of gold.

Beneath the stars, the colors blend,
In endless ways, the visions mend.
A silent swirl of night's embrace,
Unveils the wonders in time and space.

From midnight thoughts, the palette flows,
In every corner, possibility grows.
The heart beats softly in vibrant hues,
As dreams take flight on the morning dews.

A dance of colors, a whimsical tease,
Inviting the soul to wander with ease.
On this canvas of dreams, we find our place,
As wandering spirits in a boundless space.

Ethereal Scribbles and Midnight Thoughts

In shadows deep, the thoughts take flight,
A dance of ink beneath the night.
Each stroke a whisper, soft and slow,
As dreams arise, and secrets flow.

With every line, a story wakes,
Of silent hearts and hidden aches.
The paper hums, a sacred place,
Where time dissolves without a trace.

Ethereal scribbles, bright and bold,
Unravel tales yet to be told.
In midnight's grasp, we pen our fears,
And watch them fade like distant tears.

So let the ink spill freely here,
In scribbled thoughts, we find our cheer.
With every word, a truth ignites,
In quiet hours, fleeting nights.

Colors of a Daydream

In hues that blend, the sun will rise,
With strokes of gold across the skies.
A daydream floats on gentle air,
With every color, love lays bare.

Emerald greens and sapphire blue,
Each shade a hint of something true.
As rosy clouds begin to dance,
We lose ourselves in dreams of chance.

Through swirling pastels, we shall glide,
On waves of whimsy, hearts opened wide.
The canvas of a fleeting day,
In vibrations of joyful play.

Let every moment brush with light,
As daydreams weave through day and night.
In colors bright, our spirits soar,
Forever linger, asking for more.

Lines Drawn in Moonlight

By silver beams, the ink does trace,
Soft outlines of a hidden face.
In moonlit glow, the shadows play,
As dreams and secrets find their way.

With gentle curves, the stories flow,
Each whispered thought, a tender glow.
In midnight's hush, the silence sings,
A symphony of quiet things.

Upon the page, reflections gleam,
Illuminated by the dream.
Lines drawn softly, hearts laid bare,
In moonlight's warmth, we find our share.

So let the stars become our guide,
In every stroke, our souls confide.
With pen in hand, we write our fates,
And dance along the heavenly gates.

Tales of the Wandering Pen

With restless ink, the pen will roam,
From paper shores to thoughts unknown.
Each quest unfolds a new embrace,
A journey through a boundless space.

Whispers of tales, both wild and sweet,
Where dreams converge and moments meet.
The wandering pen, a trusted friend,
In every line, adventures blend.

From distant lands to skies so blue,
It sketches worlds, both old and new.
As stories spin, they intertwine,
In tapestry unbound by time.

Let ink flow free, let voices rise,
As every tale begins to fly.
The wandering pen will never tire,
Creating magic, heart's desire.

A Realm of Inspiration

In the stillness, ideas glow,
A spark ignites, feelings flow.
Words dance lightly, hearts take flight,
In a realm where dreams unite.

Among the shadows, voices sing,
Hope's gentle touch, a soaring wing.
Thoughts like rivers, deep and wide,
Guiding us to the other side.

With every whisper, visions bloom,
Casting light in the darkest room.
Bright horizons, our spirits chase,
Finding joy in each warm embrace.

So let us wander, hand in hand,
Through this vast and vibrant land.
For in this space, we truly see,
Inspiration's sweet melody.

Clouded Ambitions

Beneath the weight of twilight skies,
Plans are hidden; shadows rise.
Whispers of doubt creep in tight,
Clouded ambitions, lost from sight.

In every heartbeat, a flicker stays,
A fleeting hope in the haze.
Yet through the mist, a path appears,
Guiding the soul past fears and tears.

With every step, the clouds may part,
Revealing courage buried in the heart.
Dreams collide, and visions entwine,
Bringing clarity to the tangled line.

So we press on, though skies may weep,
Chasing dreams that dare to leap.
For within the gray, a spark still gleams,
Awakening our brightest dreams.

Dreamtextured Tangles

In tangled threads of silvered night,
Dreams entwine, both calm and bright.
Softly weaving, the mind takes flight,
In dreamtextured worlds, we find our light.

Each thought a color, vivid and bold,
Stories whispered, secrets told.
Lost in a tapestry richly spun,
Finding solace as night is done.

Visions twirl in a graceful dance,
Embracing chance, a fleeting glance.
Among the stars, where wishes sigh,
Dreams come alive, refusing to die.

So hold the magic, cherish the play,
As dawn unfolds, light leads the way.
In the weave of dreams, we shall find,
The heart's true call, forever entwined.

Woven Whispers

In the dusk, soft secrets weave,
Threads of stories that we believe.
Whispers cradled in twilight's arms,
Echoing gently, filled with charms.

In every silence, a tale awaits,
Binding souls, opening gates.
Woven whispers in the breeze,
Carrying dreams like rustling leaves.

Beneath the stars, our fears unwind,
In this tapestry, comfort we find.
With every heartbeat, the night's embrace,
We are woven in time and space.

So let us share, let our voices blend,
With woven whispers that never end.
In unity, our hearts will soar,
Finding connection forevermore.

Fantastical Forms and Fluffy Clouds

In skies where wishes twist and play,
Fluffy clouds drift and sway.
Shapes of dreams in azure bright,
Dancing softly, pure delight.

Whispers of the sunbeam's grace,
Chasing shadows, leaving trace.
Among the hues of pink and gold,
Every moment feels like bold.

Cotton castles float above,
Charmed by air and filled with love.
Imagination takes its flight,
In that realm of day and night.

Doodles of a Wandering Soul

On pages worn, the stories swirl,
With every line, a thought unfurl.
Sketches born from heart's desire,
Ink and dreams, a dance of fire.

Through winding paths of ink and tone,
A restless heart finds ways to roam.
Imprints left on pages fine,
Whispers of what may combine.

In margins wide, the laughter stays,
As doodles mark the fleeting days.
A journey traced in simple art,
The wandering soul, a work of heart.

Imprints of a Dreaming Heart

In slumber's grasp, the visions bloom,
A canvas bright, beyond the gloom.
Each heartbeat sings a vibrant song,
In the night where dreams belong.

Echoes soft, like gentle tides,
Whisper of love, where hope abides.
Moments captured, fluttering light,
In the depths of endless night.

Imprints linger, shadows cast,
Memories woven, shadows past.
In the quiet, echoes remain,
A dreaming heart, a sweet refrain.

The Art of Quiet Wonder

In the stillness, moments breathe,
Nature whispers, hearts believe.
A world unfolded, soft and pure,
In silence, mysteries endure.

The rustle leaves, the songbirds sing,
In every note, the joy they bring.
A tapestry of light and shade,
In quiet arts, the soul is laid.

The gentle touch of morning dew,
Brings forth colors, fresh and new.
In every pause, we find our truth,
The art of wonder, ageless youth.

Rhapsody in Scribbles

In the margins, dreams take flight,
Scribbles dance in the dimming light.
Whispers of thoughts in chaotic swirls,
Ink spills secrets, as the paper twirls.

A burst of colors flows with ease,
As the heart speaks through strokes and keys.
Moments captured, free and wild,
A universe formed, a blank page's child.

Symphonies written in shades of hue,
Every scribble tells a tale that's true.
Lost in the rhythm, I dare to roam,
In these verses, I find my home.

With each mark, a piece of my soul,
Captured in ink, the world feels whole.
Rhapsody sung in a paper's embrace,
In the scribbles, I find my place.

Midnight Musings

At the witching hour, thoughts collide,
Stars awaken, shadows abide.
Whispers echo in the calm of night,
Dreams take root in silvery light.

The moon, a guide through darkened skies,
Shimmers softly, as the owl cries.
Silken whispers of distant lands,
Caress my mind with gentle hands.

Words gently flutter, like moths to flame,
In the stillness, I seek no fame.
Midnight musings, a heart laid bare,
In the quietude, I breathe the air.

Through the window, thoughts intertwine,
In the night's embrace, I feel divine.
Moments woven in tapestry vast,
In each heartbeat, the night holds fast.

Fantasia of Lines

In a world where lines converge,
Creativity begins to surge.
Pencil whispers, colors sing,
A fantastical dance, the joy they bring.

Horizons stretch beyond the page,
Every stroke, a part of the stage.
Imagination soars on wings of grace,
In each line, I find my space.

Figures twirl in a vibrant blend,
As visions and reality transcend.
Brushes tap to an unseen beat,
In this fantasy, I find my seat.

From chaos born, a masterpiece,
In every corner, sweet release.
Fantasia flows, a river divine,
With each line drawn, the heart aligns.

Enchanted Inkblots

Blotted dreams upon the page,
A canvas set, a mystic stage.
Shapes emerge from shadows deep,
Inkblots gather, stories to keep.

Each splatter, a journey begun,
Colors splash, painting the sun.
Unexpected forms in lively dance,
In every drip, a hidden chance.

A world of wonder unfolds anew,
Where ink and heart craft visions true.
Enchanted moments, they intertwine,
In every blot, a glimpse divine.

The ink whispers secrets of old,
In swirls of magic, stories unfold.
Through enchanted inkblots, I see,
A universe crafted just for me.

Whimsical Whirls of Thought

In a garden of ideas, petals spin,
Every dream a ripple, where do I begin?
Curious whispers dance in the breeze,
Tickling the senses, putting minds at ease.

Clouds of whimsy drift above,
Painting the skies with gentle love.
Thoughts like butterflies, flit and twirl,
In this magical realm, the mind can whirl.

A hat full of wonders, secrets untold,
Stories unravel, both timid and bold.
Imagination's palette, colors so bright,
Sparking the night with dreams that take flight.

In this swirling vortex, let time stand still,
Each unwritten word, a heart to fill.
Whimsical whirls, a joyous dance,
Lost in the moment, a blissful trance.

Untamed Fantasies in Ink

With ink like magic, I paint the air,
Fantasies awaken, dreams laid bare.
Untamed visions take their form,
In the heart of chaos, creation's storm.

Every stroke a journey, wild and free,
Pages unfurling, what will be, will be.
A dash of madness, a splash of light,
In the depths of the paper, shadows ignite.

Whispers of freedom in every line,
Stories emerge from the depths of time.
Untamed spirits dance in the glow,
With every letter, the mind can grow.

In this inked haven, adventure calls,
A symphony of fantasies, echoing walls.
With every creation, I find my voice,
In the realm of untamed dreams, I rejoice.

Scribbles in the Moonbeam Glow

Under the moonlight, whispers ignite,
Scribbling secrets that twinkle at night.
Glows of silver wrap around thoughts,
Capturing moments that time forgot.

Lines intertwine like vines in a dream,
Wistful and soft, a gentle stream.
In the quiet, the magic unfurls,
Scribbles dancing in a world of pearls.

A canvas of stars, a shimmering sea,
Each stroke a heartbeat, alive and free.
Moonbeams guide the hand with grace,
In this luminous night, I find my place.

With every scribble, the soul unfolds,
Tales of wonder waiting to be told.
In the glow of the night, I let them go,
As dreams take flight in the moonbeam glow.

Dreamcatcher Strokes

In the night sky, dreams weave and spin,
With a gentle touch, where do I begin?
Dreamcatcher strokes, an artist's delight,
Painting the visions that take to flight.

Threads of hope intertwined with care,
Capturing wishes, floating in air.
Each line a promise, a spark of light,
Guiding the heart through the dark of night.

Winds of creativity softly call,
Inviting the spirit to rise and fall.
A tapestry woven with passion and fire,
In the dreamcatcher's net, we find desire.

Colors of dreams spiral and twine,
In this sacred space, our souls align.
With every stroke, a vision is shown,
In the heart of the dreamer, we find our home.

Creations Born from Slumber

In the quiet night so deep,
Dreams take flight where shadows creep.
Whispers dance upon the air,
Breathing life to visions rare.

Fingers trace the stars above,
Crafting tales of light and love.
From the silence, worlds arise,
Born of peace and starlit skies.

Found within a gentle sigh,
Wonders bloom and softly fly.
In this realm where time stands still,
Dreams awaken, hearts to fill.

Creating magic from a dream,
Life unfolds like a tender seam.
In the slumber, beauty gleams,
From night's depths, we weave our dreams.

Gradients of a Thoughtful Heart

In the canvas of the mind,
Colors swirl, gentle and kind.
Brushstrokes speak of hopes and fears,
Softly echo through the years.

Shades of joy blend into sorrow,
Crafting visions of tomorrow.
Every hue a tale to tell,
Of fleeting moments, lost and well.

From vibrant reds to calming blues,
Each a whisper, each a muse.
The heart paints with every breath,
Sketching life in love and death.

As the dawn greets the night,
Shadows fade in morning light.
Gradients shift, a work of art,
Captured in a thoughtful heart.

Cloud-Castle Blueprints

In a sky where dreams reside,
Clouds become a brilliant guide.
Drawn with laughter, soaked in light,
Blueprints swirl, a wondrous sight.

Structures high, where wishes dwell,
Stories whispered, tales they tell.
Glimmers of a world unknown,
From these clouds, our hopes are sewn.

Arching walls of feathery grace,
In this haven, we find our place.
With each breeze, a spark ignites,
Building castles in the heights.

Sketching dreams upon the air,
Clouds embrace without a care.
In this realm of soft delight,
Blueprints soar into the light.

Midnight Musings in Pastel Hues

As the clock strikes midnight clear,
Thoughts emerge, both soft and near.
In pastel shades, they swirl and play,
Guiding hearts till break of day.

Moments linger, gently spun,
Dreams collide, a dance begun.
Whispers held in tender tones,
Lightly drift like wandering stones.

Each idea a gentle breeze,
Carrying hopes with graceful ease.
In the stillness, visions bloom,
Painting night in soft perfume.

With every hour, new dreams arise,
Midnight's grace, under darkened skies.
Captured in these pastel hues,
Musings weave our nightly muse.

Mystical Illustrations of the Mind

Whispers of dreams in dawn's embrace,
Shadows of thoughts in a tender space.
Colors dance in a silent swirl,
Crafting worlds where ideas unfurl.

A canvas blank, yet visions gleam,
Echoes of past, woven in a dream.
With every stroke, the heart ignites,
A symphony of hidden delights.

Awakening sparks in the depths we find,
Secrets, stories, all intertwined.
Unlocking the gates of the unseen door,
Infinite realms we dare to explore.

In the gallery of the mind we tread,
Each vibrant hue a word unsaid.
With ink and paint, our souls align,
Mystical illustrations of the mind.

Flights of Fancy on Paper

With wings of whimsy, thoughts take flight,
Dancing on pages, pure delight.
Sketches of dreams float high and free,
Imagined wonders, just you and me.

A world unfurls with ink's embrace,
Sketching joy on a blank white space.
Traveling far to realms unknown,
In the garden of fantasy, we've grown.

Glimmers of laughter on every line,
Each stroke a tale, a treasure divine.
Through swirls and curves, we'll journey far,
Flights of fancy, our guiding star.

As we turn the pages, time stands still,
Crafting our stories with heart and will.
On paper's wings, let us take our chance,
In the ballet of thoughts, we shall dance.

Serenity Scrawled in Color

In gentle hues, the heart finds peace,
Colors whisper, bringing sweet release.
Brush against paper, let moments flow,
A tranquil canvas, where feelings grow.

Soft pastels blend with calming grace,
Serenity blooms in this quiet space.
Each stroke a sigh, a breath of ease,
In vibrant landscapes, our worries cease.

Through shades of blue and green we glide,
Finding solace where dreams reside.
With every layer, our spirits rise,
Serenity scrawled beneath wide skies.

A world transformed by color's might,
In every piece, a flicker of light.
Let brushes dance, let our souls collide,
In this serene space, we abide.

Lost in the World of Lines

In the labyrinth where thoughts entwine,
Every curve and angle, a woven sign.
With pencil's lead, we trace our fate,
Lost in lines that resonate.

Measured strokes create a path,
Drawing forth both joy and wrath.
In tangled webs of graphite dreams,
Flowing gently like quiet streams.

The dance of lines, both bold and fine,
Sketching the heart where secrets shine.
In shadows and light, a tale unfolds,
A story whispered, a truth retold.

With every mark, a step we take,
In this embrace, our hearts awake.
Through simple lines, we craft our view,
Lost in the world where dreams come true.

Silhouettes of Serenity

In twilight's gentle embrace,
Shadows dance in soft grace.
Whispers of a tranquil night,
Guide the stars, a soothing light.

The moon hums a lullaby,
As clouds drift slowly by.
Nature's breath, a calming breeze,
Wraps the world in quiet ease.

Silent rivers weave their tales,
Through the woods, where magic sails.
Each silhouette a story spun,
In the arms of day, now done.

With every heartbeat, peace revived,
In the stillness, souls contrived.
Underneath the sky's vast dome,
We find within, our true home.

Imaginative Whirlwinds

Thoughts swirl like autumn leaves,
In a dance that never cleaves.
Ideas burst like vibrant skies,
Coloring dreams that never die.

A canvas waits for strokes of light,
Where fantasy takes graceful flight.
Brush of dreams ignites the air,
With each whisper, free from care.

Voices echo in the wilds,
Imagination, nature's child.
Chasing shadows, spinning tales,
On the winds where freedom sails.

Through the tempest, creation's spark,
Guides us gently from the dark.
In the chaos, beauty found,
Whirlwinds sing, a joyful sound.

Scribbled Secrets

In margins worn and pages creased,
Whispered thoughts that never ceased.
Ink-stained fingers hold the key,
To shadows of the heart, set free.

Letters twine like lovers' hands,
Hidden dreams in distant lands.
Each scribble, a secret kept,
In silent echoes, promises wept.

Notes on napkins, fleeting chance,
With every stroke, a daring dance.
In the shadows of the mind,
Lies the truth that we must find.

Unraveled tales, in daylight's glow,
Scribbled whispers, soft and low.
In the quiet, truth reveals,
A world alive with what it feels.

Daydreams in Color

Brush of sun on fields of green,
In visions bright, the vibrant scene.
Underneath the azure sky,
Imaginations soar and fly.

Pinks and golds in evening's hue,
Paint the world with dreams anew.
Each thought a stroke of lively flair,
Daydreams spread, light as air.

Through painted gardens, hopes will bloom,
In swirling colors, dispel the gloom.
Every heart a canvas wide,
In daydreams, we joyfully glide.

As twilight calls the day to rest,
Color whispers, life is blessed.
In the tapestry of our dreams,
We find where love and joy redeems.

Layers of Longing

Beneath the surface, whispers sigh,
Echoes of dreams that drift and fly.
Each layer unfolds, stories untold,
In the depths of desire, a heart made bold.

Fingers trace paths on skin so fair,
Each touch ignites a longing, rare.
Veils of the past, shadows in light,
Chasing the moments, lost in the night.

A canvas of hopes, painted in tears,
Every color sings of latent fears.
In the silence, passions collide,
Layers of longing we cannot hide.

Yet within the ache, beauty finds grace,
In every heartbeat, we find our place.
In the tapestry woven, threads intertwine,
Layers of longing, forever divine.

The Art of Daydreaming

In the soft light of fading day,
Thoughts drift like clouds, float away.
Imagination paints with hues so bright,
A canvas of wonders, pure delight.

Stories unfold in a gentle breeze,
Whispers of magic among the trees.
Time slows down, allowing me to see,
The art of daydreaming sets me free.

Stars twinkle softly, inviting the night,
A realm of wishes, just out of sight.
With every dream, the soul takes flight,
Embracing the unknown, heart so light.

In the quiet corners of my mind,
Peace and adventure beautifully aligned.
The art of daydreaming, a sacred space,
Where the heart finds solace, a warm embrace.

Enigmatic Expressions

In laughter's echoes, secrets reside,
Mysteries linger, never to hide.
Eyes whisper tales that words can't convey,
Enigmatic expressions, in shadows they play.

Through the silence, a glance can ignite,
Expressions reveal what's hidden from sight.
A smile can harbor both joy and despair,
Layers of meaning linger in the air.

With every heartbeat, stories unfold,
In fragmented moments, the truth is told.
Artistry's dance on the canvas of life,
Enigmatic expressions, beauty in strife.

In the stillness, connections ignite,
With every glance, the world feels right.
In the symphony of souls, we find our way,
Expressions of enigmas, come what may.

Spirals of Serenity

In gentle whispers, peace descends,
A soft embrace, the heart mends.
Where stillness dwells, the spirit flies,
Beneath the vast and open skies.

Among the trees, the silence hums,
A symphony of nature comes.
With every breeze, a soothing tune,
A dance of light beneath the moon.

In emerald fields, the wildflowers sway,
Each petal tells a tale today.
With every step, the burden lifts,
Life's simple joys, the greatest gifts.

With every heartbeat, calm prevails,
In spirals of serene details.
The world is still, the heartbeats blend,
In spirals of serenity, we mend.

Doodles in Dreamlight

In twilight's glow, the dreams take flight,
With joyful colors, a dance of light.
Each whisper drawn, a tale unfurls,
In doodles of youth, a world of swirls.

A canvas bright, where thoughts collide,
Imagination as the joyful guide.
With gentle strokes, the shadows fall,
In dreamlight's realm, we hear the call.

The stars align in strokes so fine,
Each twinkling thought, a sacred sign.
In every scribble, laughter grows,
A melody sweet, where wonder flows.

Through pages worn, life's sketches stay,
In doodles of dreamlight, come what may.
With every glance, a memory gleams,
In the heart's gallery, live our dreams.

Inked Reveries

With ink and quill, the stories breathe,
On pages white, our souls we weave.
In every line, a journey starts,
Inked reveries from hidden hearts.

The whispers of time in every mark,
Dreams ignited, igniting sparks.
With each stroke, the past unfolds,
In tales of warmth, a world that holds.

In shadows dark, the light will find,
The dreams once lost, now intertwined.
Binding moments, in verses cast,
Inked reveries, a spell is cast.

So let the pen dance on the page,
In every story, we find our sage.
With ink that flows and hearts that dare,
Inked reveries, our truths laid bare.

Beyond the Horizon of Thought

Through endless skies, the mind will soar,
Beyond the horizon, seeking more.
In whispers soft, possibilities rise,
A journey unfolds, with open skies.

Each star a thought, a wish set free,
In the expanse of infinity.
With every heartbeat, the vision grows,
Beyond the horizon, where wonder flows.

In distant lands, the dreams align,
With every sunrise, the light will shine.
The canvas vast, where visions dance,
Beyond the horizon, a sweet romance.

So chase the dawn, let spirits glide,
In the realm of dreams, we will abide.
Beyond the horizon of thought, we find,
The echoes of the ever-expanding mind.

Whispers of Imagination

In the quiet dusk, thoughts arise,
Softly woven in the skies.
Dreams take flight, gentle and bright,
Painting shadows in the night.

A fluttering page, a heart's delight,
Words cascade like stars in flight.
Silent whispers from the deep,
Unravel secrets, softly sweep.

Visions dance in colors grand,
Crafting worlds at my command.
Each phrase a note in the air,
Echoing dreams beyond compare.

With every line, my spirit soars,
Unlocking hidden, open doors.
In the realm where wonders grow,
Imagination's endless flow.

Sketches from a Sleepy Mind

In twilight's glow, thoughts take their flight,
Sketching dreams in the soft moonlight.
A canvas of stars, brush strokes of grey,
Sleepy moments fade into play.

Waves of slumber gently tease,
Creating calm, a soothing breeze.
Lines of whimsy intertwine,
In echoes where the shadows shine.

Pencil trails on pages bare,
Whispers of what lingers there.
A lullaby in shades of blue,
Capturing visions, fresh and new.

With every sketch, my dreams awake,
Breath of wonder, softly quake.
Painting night in layers deep,
A journey spun from thoughts of sleep.

Fantasies on Paper's Edge

On paper's edge, where dreams collide,
Fantasies pulse like an ocean's tide.
Colors blend in vibrant hues,
Crafting tales of wondrous views.

With every word, worlds expand,
Imagination's quiet hand.
Each line a step in the unknown,
A realm of magic, all my own.

In simple strokes, stories unfold,
Adventures waiting to be told.
Whispers of truth in every glance,
Life and dreams in a tender dance.

On paper's edge, my heart will roam,
Transforming thoughts into a home.
A sanctuary where I can seep,
Into the fantasies I keep.

Strokes of a Starry Night

Under a sky of endless pitch,
Stars embroider, bright and rich.
Each twinkle writes a tale above,
In strokes of silver, dreams of love.

The moon dips low, a tender glance,
Inviting night to start its dance.
Whispers drift on velvet air,
Hopes entwined in the night's fair hair.

Brushstrokes swirl as shadows glide,
Capturing magic, far and wide.
In the cool embrace of the night,
Imagination takes its flight.

With every stroke, the stars ignite,
Painting stories of pure delight.
Under a cloak of midnight's charm,
The world awakes, serene and warm.

Milton Keynes UK
Ingram Content Group UK Ltd.
UKHW021629011224
451755UK00010B/520